STORIES FROM
✝ ✝ ✝ ✝ *the* ✝ ✝ ✝ ✝
CHRISTIAN
WORLD

Written by **David Self**

Illustrated by **Sheena Vickers**

MACDONALD YOUNG BOOKS

First published in Great Britain in 1998
by Macdonald Young Books,
an imprint of Wayland Publishers Ltd

Macdonald Young Books
61 Western Road
Hove
East Sussex
BN3 1JD

Find Macdonald Young Books on the
internet at: http://www.myb.co.uk

Text © David Self 1986

Illustration by Sheena Vickers
© Macdonald Young Books 1998

Editor: Rosie Nixon

Designer: Dalia Hartman

A CIP catalogue record for this book is
available from the British Library

ISBN 0 7500 2554 9

Printed and bound in Portugal by

Edições ASA

CONTENTS

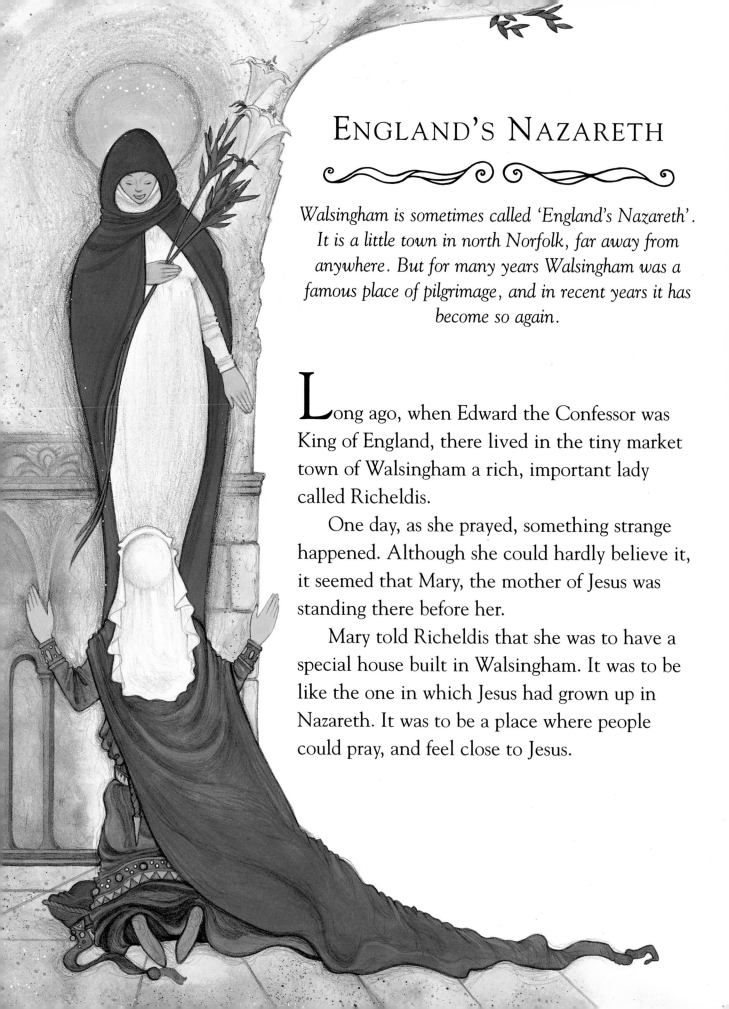

ENGLAND'S NAZARETH

Walsingham is sometimes called 'England's Nazareth'. It is a little town in north Norfolk, far away from anywhere. But for many years Walsingham was a famous place of pilgrimage, and in recent years it has become so again.

Long ago, when Edward the Confessor was King of England, there lived in the tiny market town of Walsingham a rich, important lady called Richeldis.

One day, as she prayed, something strange happened. Although she could hardly believe it, it seemed that Mary, the mother of Jesus was standing there before her.

Mary told Richeldis that she was to have a special house built in Walsingham. It was to be like the one in which Jesus had grown up in Nazareth. It was to be a place where people could pray, and feel close to Jesus.

At first, Richeldis was not sure what to do. Then Mary appeared to her again, and again – with the same message. Richeldis arranged for builders and carpenters to start work. But where was the house to be built?

As Richeldis considered this, a spring of water suddenly burst out of the ground. It became a well, and there they built a house. People did come to pray and, while they were there, they felt they were in the company of Jesus. People who were ill found that if they drank the water or bathed in it, they were often cured. Walsingham soon became famous, with visitors coming from all over Europe.

That was all a long time ago. Many years later, the house was pulled down by wicked men. People forgot where it had been. But just over fifty years ago, a new holy house was begun. As the builders started to clear the ground for it, they found an ancient well. They cleared it out – and it quickly filled with pure water!

Once again people started to visit Walsingham, some to be healed, some just to pray and to feel close to Jesus, in England's Nazareth.

VOICES

The French called her Jeanne la Poucelle (Joan the Maid); the English called her Joan of Arc. To the French, she was a heroine. To the English, she was a witch. Her story began in the year 1425, when England and France were at war.

J oan was an ordinary country girl, about thirteen years old. But after that summer's day she would never be ordinary again.

She was in the garden, when she heard the voices. They seemed to come from a blaze of light. At first she was frightened, but then she became convinced they were angel voices.

One was the archangel, Michael. What was he saying?
She must become a soldier and help the young king
of France to win the war against the English!

How could a farmer's daughter do that? She did nothing.
Perhaps the voices would stop. They didn't. She told her
family and friends about them. They were amazed.

At last she left home and went to see the local nobleman.

'I'm called Joan,' she said. 'I come from the village of
Domremy and I've been told to save France from the English,
so please will you give me a suit of armour, a horse and help
me get to the king?'

'Why should I believe you?' he asked.

'Because our army is about to be defeated again.'

A few minutes later, came news of that defeat.

The nobleman sent her to the king.
He believed her story and sent her on
to the commander of the army,
a man called Dubois.

At that time, part of the French army was trapped in the city of Orleans. The English army was surrounding the city on three sides. On the fourth side was a river. How could the French be rescued?

'Simple,' said Joan. 'We get boats and cross the river and save the town.'

'I've got the boats,' said Dubois. 'But the wind's blowing the wrong way. See?'

'Oh! is that all? I'll go to church and pray,' said Joan, walking away.

When she got back, the wind had changed. The boats crossed the river, and the two parts of the French army were able to link up and save Orleans.

FRANCIS OF ASSISI

One of the kindest and most loved Christians of all time must be St Francis. He was born in the town of Assisi in northern Italy, the son of a rich tradesman. As a young man, he gave away all he owned and tried to live as Jesus had done.

Peter Bernardone was furious. It was all to do with his boy, Francis (who was really no longer a boy, but a young man). Peter Bernardone was very rich. He wanted young Francis to enjoy the same sort of life as the wealthy young noblemen of the town. That way, he thought, the family would be respected and feared by the ordinary people.

At first, Francis enjoyed going to parties and spending money. His father was satisfied.

But then, Francis was ill for a while. As he got better, he started to spend more time on his own, praying. Whenever he could, he gave his money and food to the poor and needy. He no longer wore fine, expensive clothes.

One day, he was praying in a church called St Damian's, just outside Assisi. The church was rather old and almost in ruins. As Francis prayed, the crucifix in the church seemed to speak to him: 'Francis, repair my church.'

Now, Peter Bernardone was away on business. Francis went back home, took some of his father's goods and sold them. Then he took the money to the priest at St Damian's, to pay for the repairs. And that was why Peter Bernardone was furious. He took his son to see the bishop, and told him the whole story.

The bishop listened to the tale. Turning to Francis he said gently, 'Francis, the Church cannot take what does not belong to it. You must give back to your father what is his.'

So Francis took the money and gave it back to his father. Then he started taking off his clothes and throwing them at him. 'Now I owe you nothing, Father!' he said as he took off the very last of them. 'You are no longer my father and I have no father but my Father in Heaven.'

Peter Bernardone took his money and stormed out. Someone put an old workman's tunic around Francis. His new life had begun.

BROTHERS AND SISTERS

From that day, Francis lived very simply, owning nothing and eating only the food he could beg. Others joined him and they became known as Franciscans. Among other things, Francis became famous for his love for animals and birds. This is one of the stories later told about that love.

'What God wants us to do is –' said Francis.
'We can't hear you!' interrupted the people.
It was true. They couldn't.

There was Francis, standing on a little hill, talking to a crowd of people. And the reason they couldn't hear him was because a large number of swallows were building nests nearby and chirping very loudly.

'My dear sister swallows,' said Francis, 'you have said enough! Listen to the word of God and be quiet till I have finished.'

To everyone's amazement, the swallows all settled on the edges of the buildings and in trees, and were silent.

'Thank you,' said Francis. 'As I was saying, what God wants us to do is to love each other. Be kind to each other. We are all brothers and sisters – even the animals and birds. That is why I call the swallows "sisters"...'

And the swallows kept silent until he had finished teaching. Then, once again, they began to sing.

SET FREE IN FREETOWN

On June 29, 1864 in Canterbury Cathedral, a man called Samuel Adjai Crowther became the first black African to be made a bishop. It was thanks to him that many people in Nigeria first heard about Jesus.

Adjai grew up in the Land of the Yoruba River in what is now Nigeria. He lived life like any other boy until one terrible day he was kidnapped.

A group of strange white men came to his village. Quickly and roughly, they seized Adjai. He was marched to the river and thrown in a boat with some other boys and young men. They were taken down the river towards the sea where a much larger ship was waiting. Soon they were prisoners in the dark depths of that ship's hold. Adjai did not know what would happen.

If he had known, he might have been even more frightened. These men were 'slavers'. They captured strong young Africans, took them by ship across the Atlantic Ocean and sold them as slaves in South America. It was against the law – but that didn't stop them. Something did, though.

Ships of the British Navy patrolled the west coast of Africa, trying to catch the slave ships as they left the African coast. Adjai was lucky. The ship he was on was stopped and all the Africans on it were taken to a port called Freetown where they were all set free.

Adjai was taken care of by a schoolmaster. He learned to read and write and heard about Jesus. He decided to become a Christian and from then he was known as Samuel Adjai Crowther.

'God has been good to me,' he said. 'So now I must work for him.' So he studied to become a priest and then translated the Bible into the Yoruba language, so that his own people could read it for themselves.

Then he went back to the Land of the Yoruba and travelled by boat along its rivers. He stopped at the villages to tell the people about Jesus. They respected him and believed what he taught – and Adjai never forgot to be grateful to God.

HOME FOR THE DYING

Agnes was twelve when she decided she wanted to be a nun when she grew up. When she was thirty-six she left her convent to work in the slums of Calcutta. The name she had chosen when she became a nun was Teresa.

For eighteen years, Mother Teresa had been a nun, teaching in a school in Calcutta in India. She lived in a convent surrounded by beautiful gardens.

One day in 1946, while she was on a train journey, she seemed to hear Jesus speaking to her. 'I heard the call to give up all and follow him into the slums, to serve him among the poorest of the poor.'

She got permission to leave the convent and, with some other nuns, started a school for the very poorest children in Calcutta.

Some years later, in one of the dirtiest and poorest streets of Calcutta, she came across a woman lying in the street, dying. She was so feeble that her body had been partly eaten away by rats and ants. Mother Teresa carried her to a hospital. Reluctantly (because she was so near to dying), they took the old woman in and she was able to die in peace.

Calcutta was full of people like that. Mother Teresa knew she must help them. She got permission to use a building which had once been a Hindu temple as a 'Home for the Dying'.

Since then, until her death, Mother Teresa and her helpers took in over 36,000 dying, homeless people.

Once she told how she picked a little feeble old woman out of a dustbin. The woman said her son had put her there to die. 'We took her home to our place and we helped her. After a few hours she died in great peace.' Mother Teresa called dying 'going home'.

Of course, some of the people they helped got better. Some went to live in a comfortable home. Others even became strong enough to work again. But what Mother Teresa and her helpers wanted most was to let homeless, sick and dying people know that there is someone who loves them, someone who *wants* them. Mother Teresa's helpers continue to assist all who are in need: not just Christians, but Hindus, Muslims and Sikhs. All are welcome.

Many people have admired Mother Teresa. She won the Nobel Prize and the Pope gave her a special prize for her work. But she said it was not 'her' work. She was simply continuing the work of Jesus: helping the hungry, the sick and the homeless.

CROOKED NOSE

In the Italian city of Naples at the end of the Second World War, there were hundreds of homeless young boys. They spent their lives begging, stealing, fighting and sleeping in the streets. Always on the move, they became known as the 'scugnizzi', the 'spinning tops'.

'I'm the gang leader,' said Fatty to the young stranger. 'And who are you?'

There was a pause. Then the newcomer spat in Fatty's face and, putting his hands in his pocket, stood there defiantly.

Fatty grinned and pulled a razor-sharp knife from his pocket. 'I'd have cut you up if you hadn't been quicker to get your hand to your knife. You'd better join my gang.'

They were all known by nicknames. They called him Crooked Nose. He never let on that, on that first night, his pocket had been empty: he had no knife. Nor did he say that he was not really a homeless urchin, but a priest.

Father Mario Borrelli had just become a priest. And he'd decided he must help the scugnizzi of Naples who suffered so much from cold, hunger and illness, while the younger ones were regularly beaten up by the older ones. His plan was to make a home for them. But he knew they were afraid of priests, just as much as they were of the police. So every night he disguised himself in filthy old clothes and roamed the streets with Fatty's gang.

Meanwhile some other priests and friends were repairing and cleaning a disused church. They built a kitchen in it and collected blankets and old beds. Then, one of these helpers visited the gang to try to persuade them to come to the church.

'Priests! We're not going to get mixed up with them,' said one of the gang.

'No harm in trying,' said Crooked Nose.

Because they trusted him, they went. More came the next night. The House of the Urchins was a success. One day, Father Borrelli wore his priest's clothes while he was with the boys. They realized then that Father Borrelli was also Crooked Nose. But they didn't feel they'd been tricked. No, they knew he'd suffered, just to help them.

BACKGROUND NOTES

ENGLAND'S NAZARETH

Richeldis de Faverches was lady of the manor of Walsingham. Her 'holy house' was built in 1061 and within a century, became an important shrine of Christianity. Pilgrims visited it until 1538, when Henry VIII, who had earlier made the pilgrimage himself, ordered that the shrine should be destroyed. But in 1921 the then parish priest, Alfred Hope Patten, had a statue of Mary made. Pilgrims began coming to Walsingham once again. The new holy house was built in 1931, inside a new church.

VOICES

Joan is also known as 'the Maid', or Joan of Arc. She was born in Domremy in the Lorraine at the beginning of the 15th century. She said at first that the voices she heard came in a blaze of light – though later she said she heard them when church bells rang. She helped re-capture Orleans in 1429.

But the French were divided among themselves, and in 1430 she was captured by the faction fighting for the Duke of Burgundy, who was opposed to the king. She was burned at the stake as a witch in Rouen on May 31, 1431. She was made a saint in 1920.

FRANCIS OF ASSISI

Francis was born in 1182. The turning point of his life (described in *Francis of Assisi*) was in 1206. He then left his family and travelled with eleven followers to Rome. In 1215, the Pope allowed him to set up a new order of monks, called friars. Franciscan friars give up all personal possessions and try to live very simple and humble lives. Francis taught that we should love and care for all of God's creation.

He died in 1226. Two years later he was canonized – which means that from then on he was known as St Francis.

SET FREE IN FREETOWN

Adjai Crowther was captured when only a child, and seemed destined for slavery in America. Instead, he was 'set free in Freetown', in Sierra Leone. There he received some education and was then sent to school for a time in London. He returned to Sierra Leone, and later became a priest. He went back to his homeland (in what is now Nigeria) to teach his own people about Christianity, and eventually became the first black bishop, in 1864.

HOME FOR THE DYING

Mother Teresa was still at school when she heard about a group of nuns working in India. She joined them in 1929, when she was 19. She left the convent after 18 years, and started first, a school for the poorest children in Calcutta and later, the Home for the Dying. The nuns who worked with Mother Teresa were known as the Sisters of Charity. Mother Teresa died on 5 September 1997, but the good work of the Sisters of Charity continues.

CROOKED NOSE

At the end of World War II, gangs of homeless young men and boys roamed the streets of Naples. Father Borrelli – who had only recently been made a priest – set out to win their confidence and trust, and to provide a home for them in a disused church. Since then, a new home, school and clinic have been built.